The Days Of Halloween

A Pictures Book By John Rose

A FrankenGeek Press/Monster Shop Studios "THING"

PUBLISHED BY FRANKENGEEK PRESS
BOOK DESIGN & PRODUCTION BY MONSTER SHOP STUDIOS
PRINTED IN THE UNITED STATES OF AMERICA

ISBN: 0-9771182-4-X
ISBN-13: 978-0-9771182-4-3

FIRST EDITION OCTOBER 2017

Other books by John Rose:

The MonsterGrrls Series

Book 1: Out From The Shadows
Book 2: Full Moon Fever

INTRODUCTION

So.

One may wish to know how this book came about. I blame several people, but it initially started because of Greg West.

Like me, he majored in art in college, where we met and quickly discovered we were kindred spirits. After college I went on to teach in Greenwood, MS, while he gained a degree in graphic design and went on to a prestigious job designing T-shirts for fraternity and sorority parties at a print shop in Cleveland, MS. He met his lovely wife Kay, fathered two children and soon left living in the middle of nowhere in Cleveland to move with his family to the middle of nowhere in Wesson, MS. That is not anything against him; it's just that Mississippi has a great deal of middle of nowhere in general. People go on at length about the plains of Oklahoma and the deserts of Arizona and the great wide open of Texas, but for sheer unused space no other state in the Union can beat Mississippi.

We primarily keep in touch with each other through Facebook, as nearly everybody who is everybody does these days. Neither of us has had a use for Twitter, because we are from the South. If a person from the South is trying to say something in 140 characters or less, he is either ill, losing consciousness, or perhaps he is dead and trying to speak to you through an Ouija board.

Greg kept his hand in artwork by committing to art challenges on Facebook and produced a number of good and very inspired pieces. After watching him awhile, I decided that I wanted to have a go at this sort of thing, but was unsure where to start. What I saw happening, initially, was me getting sidetracked in some way, losing control of the thing and then ending up rushing to finish the several unfinished drawings I was behind on.

Eventually, October of 2015 rolled around and a photo for a "Drawlloween Challenge" popped up on Facebook. There was a different theme for each day in October, and the goal was to do one drawing per day centered around that day's theme. I decided that I would do some gag cartoons, and so began this little journey. And one of my major supporters in this journey was Greg West, who cheered me on. He's one of the reasons you are now reading this book.

Another reason you are reading this book is Claudia White, who also lives in Greenwood and is another artist friend of mine. We became friends and artistic partners in crime back in 1996, and she is important because she cheered me on and supported me even when she didn't get the ideas I had. She has been and continues to be a major source of support and inspiration for me. We do not keep in touch on Facebook, though, mainly because she has no use for Facebook, and when people ask her if she's on Twitter she laughs very loudly. But we don't need an electronic source to keep in touch because we see each other every day, which is how she was able to laugh so hard at some of the cartoons.

This book is a tribute to my love of Halloween and the Halloween season, which for me begins the major holidays of the year. In addition to the original 31 drawings, there are some new ones here that are now seeing the dark of night for the first time. I hope you enjoy them, and I wish a very Happy Halloween to you and yours indeed.
There you go.

--J. R.

THE ARTIST'S STATEMENT OF INTENT

You people don't want to waste your time reading this, and I don't want to waste *my* time by writing it.

How about we just skip to the cartoons?

"Where do you keep the *scary* costumes?"

"Of course we're serious, sir.
Would you care to take a look at our catalog?"

Goblin selfies

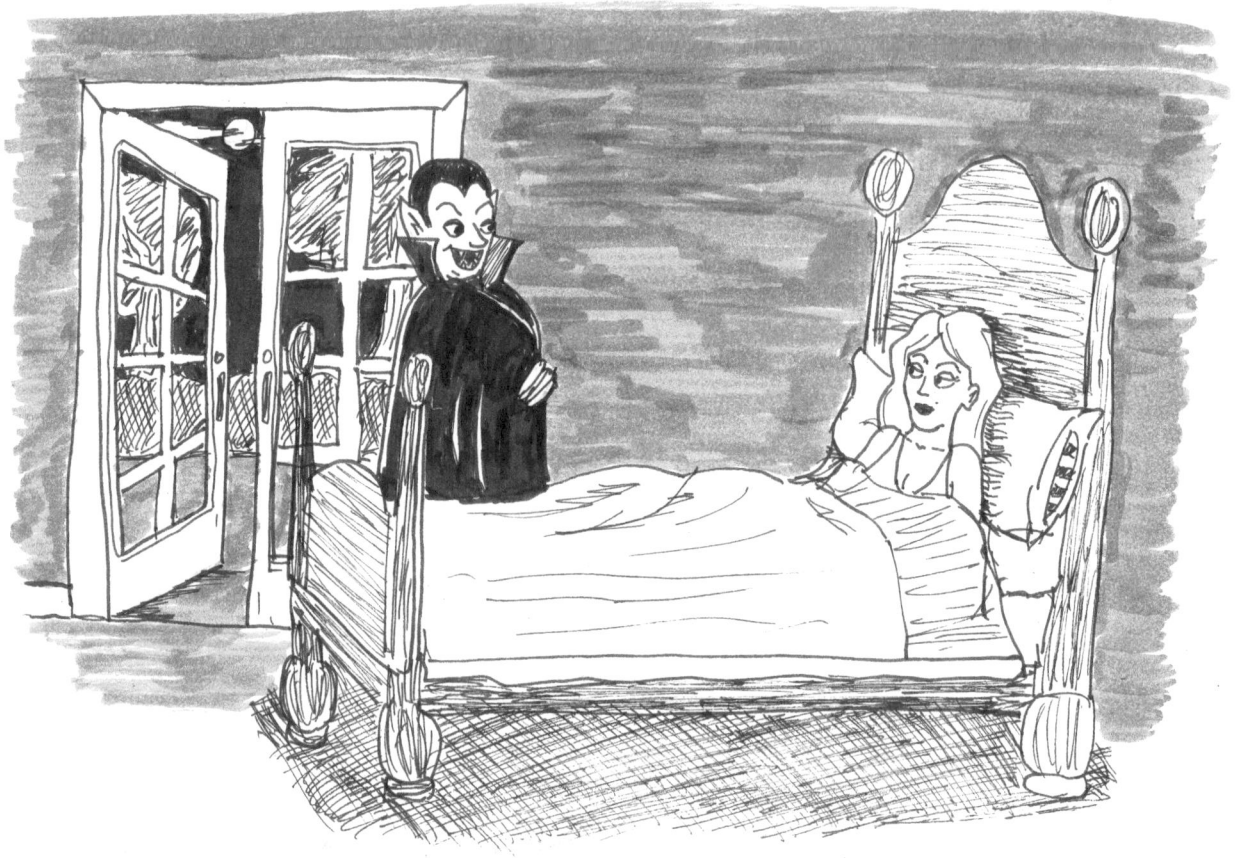

"Well, here we are again..."

"I don't think Jenkins takes the occult seriously."

"No, I'm just on my way to bridge club meeting."

"Do you know what kind of bait he used?"

"Oh, I don't know. I think it's rather romantic."

"I don't want to work with him. He overacts!"

"This is why I don't like getting ice cream. It's *terrible* when you get brain freeze!"

"I got a rock!"

"Amontillado, please."

"Get off my lawn!"

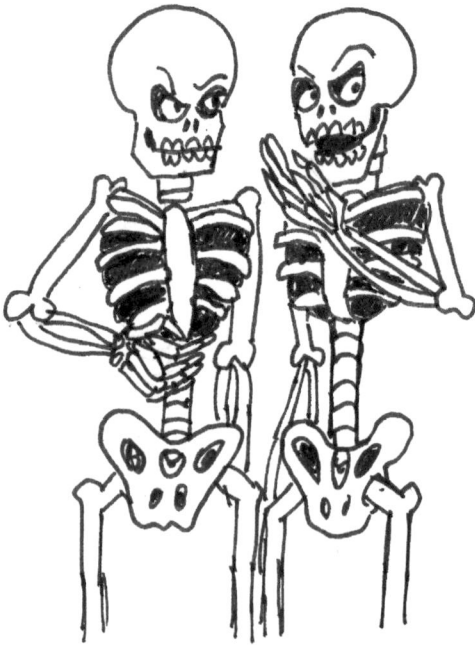

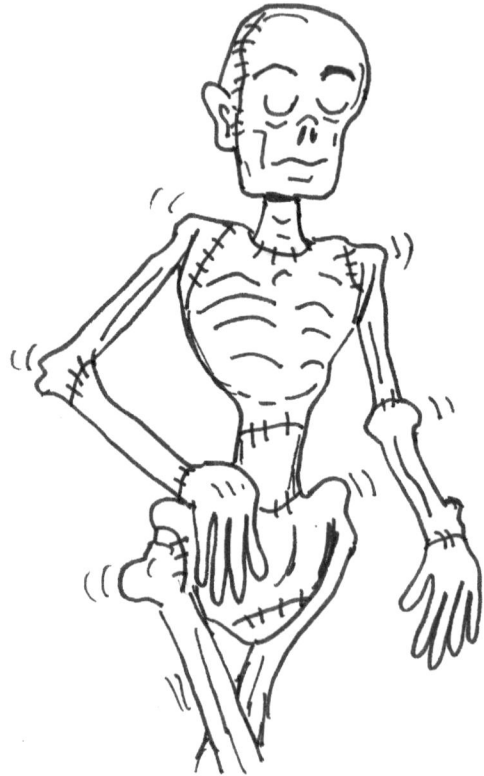

"*Someone's* had some *work* done."

"Trick or treat, eh?"

"I'm telling you, Phil spends too much time at that coffee shop."

"Revolution *now*!!"

"Don't mind him. He's been acting like that
ever since he started hanging around that writer."

"This Halloween business they do is a hell of a thing, isn't it?"

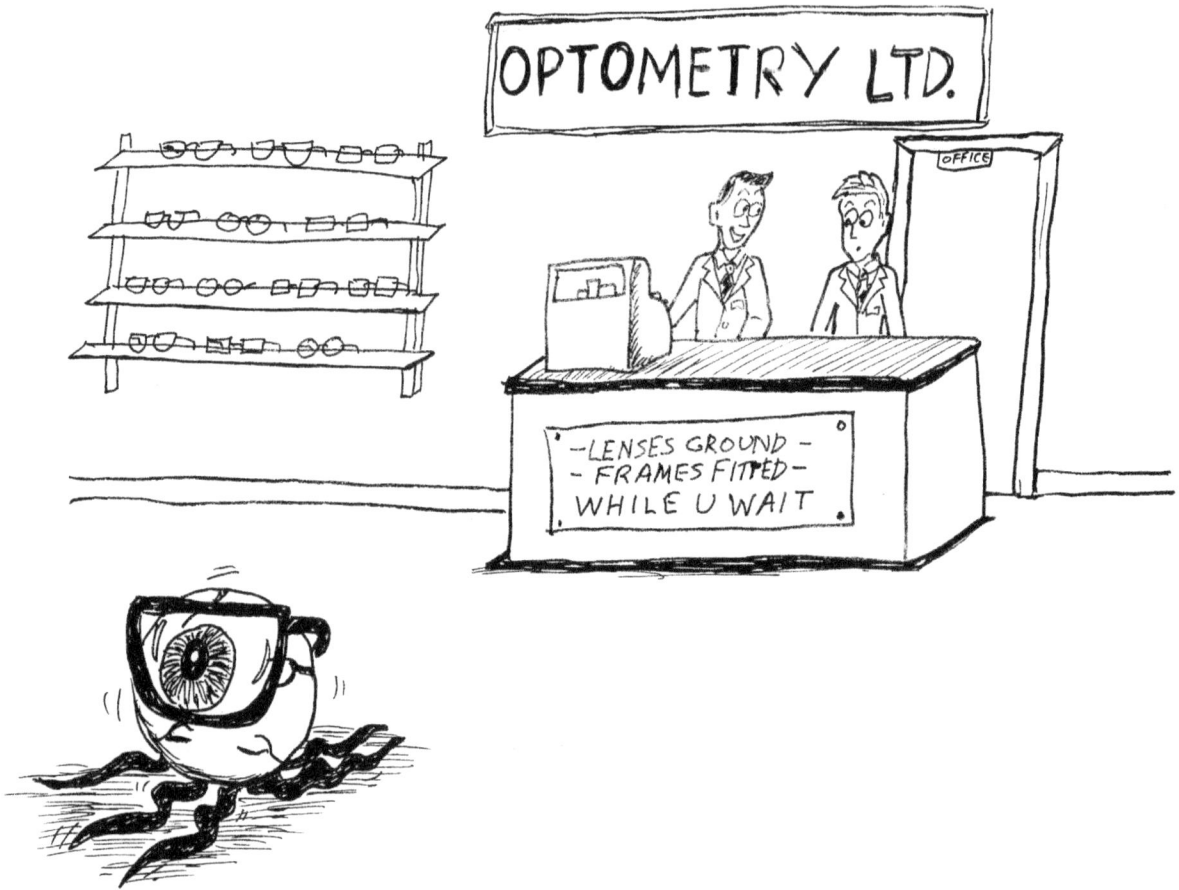

"You know, I'm just really feeling *good* right now."

"A man can dream, can't he?"

"I don't know. Between the Internet, international terrorism and reality television, it just seems like we just aren't *necessary* anymore."

"I hear it's *terrifying*."

"I don't know anything about gluten. I'm an all-liquids man myself."

"I'm sensing a fundamental breakdown
in communications with you two."

"I don't see how giving him a bib and a set of chopsticks
has improved the situation."

"No, I appreciate it. You fellas know how to make an old broad
feel good."

"It sounds like you got really turned around. But if you're OK with dried venison, you can have some of that."

"No, I'm afraid not. In my current situation, I don't
get to see a lot of movies."

"Call this a bandage, do you?"

"I wanna drink of O-positive."

"That's ridiculous! I never did *that!*"

"I see by the obituaries that Elmer Hodgkiss is going to be buried here. *That* should liven up the neighborhood..."

"Well, you guys are doing such a great job of screwing up the planet, we just figured we'd go into business for ourselves. Coffee?"

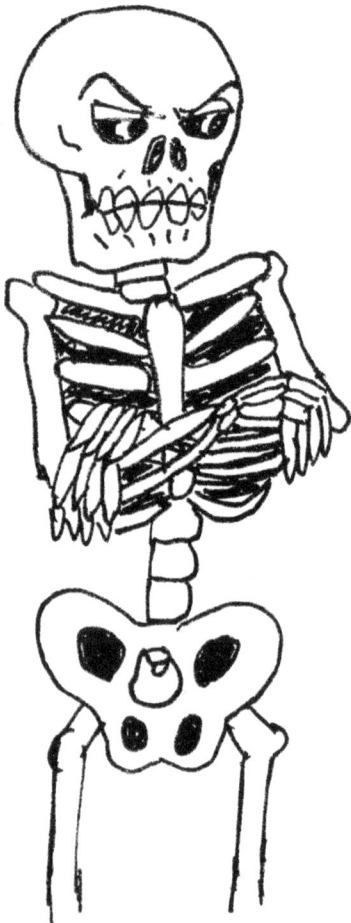

"I don't *care* if I'm not Mexican—it makes me feel *pretty!*"

"It was supposed to bring out *inner* beauty!"

"Are you kidding? Of *course* I'm doing it. You wait a whole *lifetime* for an experience like this!"

"That's right—ruin the neighborhood!"

"Yes, things are tough all over for zombies. We have friends in Washington, D.C., and they're *starving* to death."

"No, we couldn't. He's an old soppy, really,
and besides he's saving us a fortune in heating bills."

"What can you do? He's *family*."

"I *told* you. No one thinks
getting a rock for trick-or-treat is *funny*."

AFTERWORD:
I OFTEN DREAM OF HALLOWEEN

So.

Fall has come. It's chilly outside, the weather where I live has become habitable, and we have already made the first batch of chili and started talk of an experiment with beef and barley soup. And it's October. Halloween is in the distance waving hello.

I love Halloween. For me, it is the advent of a social season among my friends and me, which leads to lots of days off from work, social gathering and feasting, and hearty peasant food that often gets relegated to the winter because most of it is served hot (and in the South, you just DON'T want a lot of hot food in the summer no matter how much you may love it). Halloween leads to Thanksgiving, which leads to Christmas, which leads to New Year's.

And unfortunately, Halloween gets a bad rap. Despite the fact that we have come to celebrate Halloween much more elaborately than we used to (with times as bad as they are, we'll take any excuse for a party we can get), Halloween still has to deal with its bad reputation of pagan beginnings, mysterious things, and spooks and monsters. Halloween, its decriers say, is an Evil Holiday.

So here are my thoughts on Halloween:

My Halloween is not very pagan. I am aware of all the various forms of occult hinkiness in Halloween's past, but my Halloween is not about pentagrams, sacrifices, rituals, big stone circles, guys in white robes who look like Gandalf, or goats. In fact, I do not invite goats to Halloween parties simply because of their tendency to eat all the food at the table and then start on the tablecloth. Any goats who wish to come will have to stay on the lawn.

My Halloween is not about serial killers, hyperactive zombies, inhuman mental or physical torture, or excessive gore of the sort that is often created with a lot of latex rubber and red syrup. It is also much more inclusive and optimistic in its outlook than these genres tend to be. Nor is it concerned with a lot of dreary exposition on How Self-Destructive Bastards Human Beings Are, Especially Those Damn Republican Ones (which, more often than not, is just another way of extending your sniggering adolescent nihilism well past your forties).

My Halloween is not particularly Wiccan. I suppose all that getting back to nature and being One With The Universe is a fine thing for those who want it, but I maintain, as I always have, that the main thrust of human civilization is not to return to nature but to get as far away from it as possible. Plus, if you scratch a certain type of Wiccan hard enough you will eventually find an Earth-Motherly sort who wears Birkenstocks a lot and is trying to cut a deal with Pottery Barn to market her own line of handmade ceramics. (If I have offended any Wiccans by making that statement, I am sorry, but the Pyramid Collection catalog has made it very difficult for me to take you seriously anymore.)

My Halloween has a soft heart and a kindly attitude for monsters: Frankenstein monsters, vampires, werewolves, mummies, ghosts, witches, giant apes, Godzilla, Jekyll and Hyde, Blackie Lagoon, the Phantom of the Opera, and so on. Any of these who stalk up to the door expecting to scare someone are usually surprised and somewhat pleased to have drinks shoved in their hands (or claws, paws, appendages, etc.) and taken around to be introduced to the other guests.

My Halloween is a bit like the Addams Family's theory of entertaining: Everyone is always welcome, and if you can stand the weirdness you will most likely get asked back.

My Halloween likes vampires: not the Beautiful Prom Squad of the Twilight Saga, nor the cold supermodels of True Blood and Underworld, but the dudes who sleep in coffins, wear capes, live in castles and turn into bats. Now, granted, one of these at a modern Halloween party is a bit like Granddad figuring out the X-Box, but so what? They dress better, behave in a gentlemanly/ladylike manner, and have learned something other than how to look expensively pretty in the course of their unlives. Besides, I'd rather hang out with Bela Lugosi than Edward Whatshisname anyway.

My Halloween likes werewolves. See the above and fill in the blanks yourself.

My Halloween is truly and madly and deeply and hopelessly and unrepentantly in love with Universal Monsters, Hammer Films, and Full Moon Pictures. And at this point I want to give a shout-out to the great unsung star of almost every Hammer monster movie ever made. Not Peter Cushing, not Christopher Lee, not Oliver Reed, not all those great English character actors like Michael Gough and Barbara Steele, but... *The Candlestick*. That's right. The Candlestick turns up in just about every one of those old Hammer monster movies. Anyone who does not believe me is invited to watch any three Christopher Lee Dracula films back-to-back.

My Halloween is not truly Halloween unless there is chocolate involved at some point.

My Halloween thinks it's a damn outrage that the Great Pumpkin never made it to Linus's pumpkin patch, or that Charlie Brown spent the whole night trick-or-treating and got nothing, *nothing,* but a bagful of damned rocks. What kind of Halloween Scrooge gives a kid, *any* kid, a *rock* in their trick-or-treat bag?

My Halloween thinks the whole thought process behind Dia De Los Muertos, the business of celebrating and remembering your loved dead, is a wonderful idea.

My Halloween would never, ever, ever, *ever* put a razor blade in an apple and give it to a kid. Not even if it's that sweaty little kid from down the block who screams and howls and rides his bike across the lawn and generally acts like he's been raised by wild dingoes.

My Halloween will dress in a funky sexy costume, but is not given to overt sluttiness. It used to be that we dressed up like things we were afraid of. If the new crop of Halloween costumes is any indication, we as a people are frightened of sex, prison, zombies, organized crime, and the type of sight gag that usually shows up in any movie with "Movie" in the title. In that order.

My Halloween, while acknowledging that some of Martha Stewart's ideas are interesting, is not about in any way, shape or form to glitter a whole damn skeleton. Nor is it going to pay about $300 for one, either.

My Halloween believes in wonder and magic and kindhearted anarchy. Anyone who has ever taken a moment to stand back and look at the world around them, who has spent some time looking at pictures in a museum, or who has watched animals and people interact with each other knows that just like in *When Good Ghouls Go Bad,* there are worlds beyond this world, times beyond this time, and that the dance is never really over. We celebrate Halloween to remind ourselves of things like this: not because we want to see ghosts and monsters and magic, but because we want to imagine, for just a little while, what these things might be like. The darkness of Halloween is momentary, and sometimes even a comfort when compared to the real horrors present in the world. But love, and the soul, and the spirit abide. They are what is left when the dust is swept away.

There you go.

Happy Halloween, everybody.

--J. R.

October, 2017

About The Author

John Rose is the creator of not only this book but also the *MonsterGrrls* series. His day job is teaching art in Greenwood, MS, where he lives with three cats, a number of gargoyles and skeletons, a werewolf who lives under the house and a brain named Alfred, who lives in a jar.

Visit him and the Grrls on the Internet at http://www.monstergrrls.com.

Thanks for reading.

Dedication

For my mother, who left this world on Dec. 31, 2016.